The Kerosene Singing

The Kerosene Singing

Alistair Noon

Nine
Arches
Press

The Kerosene Singing
Alistair Noon

ISBN: 978-0-9931201-6-9

Copyright © Alistair Noon
Cover artwork © Eleanor Bennett
www.eleanorleonnebennett.com

All rights reserved. No part of this work may be reproduced, stored or transmitted in any form or by any means, graphic, electronic, recorded or mechanical, without the prior written permission of the publisher.

Alistair Noon has asserted his right under Section 77 of the Copyright, Designs and Patents Act 1988 to be identified as the author of this work.

First published October 2015 by:

Nine Arches Press
PO Box 6269
Rugby
CV21 9NL
United Kingdom

www.ninearchespress.com

Printed in Britain by:
The Russell Press Ltd.

Contents

The Expectation	11
Introduction to a Congress	13
Your Collages	14
A Note on the Door in the Land of No Phones	15
The New Village	16
Riding Home with Michel Foucault	17
We sleep inside four circled walls,	19
Le Monde diplomatique	20
About a Country	21
At Haifa	22
Khakassian Masks	23
Oblast	27
The Milan Duomo	28
Great Uncle in the Great Unknown	29
Ode on a Bottle of Maotai	30
Shanxi Tune	31
The Burbage Valley	33
The British Museum	35
From the Annals	37
The Ex-Pat Gift Shop Owner Sells Up	38
They Flick The Lights Back On	39
The Transsylvanians at Supamolly, Berlin, 7 Jan 2012	41
The Sock Exchange	43
Salat Komplett	44
The Courtyard	46
Fixing a Clock	47
An Update on the Status of Frost	48
Disturbance	49
The Financial Ocean	50

The Travellers	52
Meeting the Family	54
The fuzzy dashes fuzzy dots	56
Nobody's Mate	57
The Forester leads beneath the trees,	59
The Shelves	60
Escape	61

The Expectation

1

I see us hiking through a veering gorge,
the scrub stuck to the sides, above us goats,
their meet-and-bleat event at this convention
of herd and human. Coastal ridges loom
behind us, way beyond what we can walk,
although we'll ride where other riders rode.

2

As is our habit, we'll get ourselves lost
hunting a track that thins back into scrub
and face a king whose lands we'll have to pass,
growling and grinning, standing his ground,
the bastard, whose existence feeds on force.
We'll have to retreat from his speaking power.

3

And through the thorny undergrowth we'll forge
a route, although those nibs will jot their notes
on our skin. Nature's thought up harsh inventions;
we're going to meet them and perhaps our doom.
Meanwhile, we hope to spot the local hawk
and catch the nightingale tune of the toad.

4

We won't, I hope, have much to say to frost.
A summer is the time to rucksack up,
be on your way, remove your office arse
from its roundabout chair, and planet-bound
put off en masse accumulated chores,
to stop and spot the unrecorded flowers.

5

Turn off the lights and did you pack the torch?
An anchored platform or a barrel as it floats
out on the Black Sea's surface tension
might hum new notes or a familiar tune.
Surely there's got to be at least a stork,
its helipad visible from the road?

6

There might be monuments for us to accost,
for us to say how much we love them, rub
and stroke their sides, although they never asked
our paws to land and leap about them. Our sound
will never reach their stony ears, of course.
Their silence, though, gets through to ours.

7

Gold teeth will flash across a woman's porch
as we float in like harbour-seeking boats.
There'll be no need to ask about her pension,
her face will speak the dialect of spare rooms.
Once the price has stopped its bobbing, she'll talk
about the rent for her resort abode.

8

Beds and tents, train seats where we're booked to doss,
our shapes leave your shapes as we rev up
and move, and what seemed slow will seem as fast
as grass rising across a burial mound.
We'll hear and not hear the impending hordes.
The forecast is for thunderstorms and showers.

Introduction to a Congress

Now the lights on the walls are down,
will you give me your minute or three?
I trust your skirts and trousers
have introduced themselves to the plush seats.

As you can see, I can't see you,
and I'm blinking down at my script.
But before we hoist up our speakers,
if you need to abandon this ship

to banish your ballast and waste,
for smokes and smirks, or for plans,
our staff will light up your way
like the path of a spotlit Lancaster.

"Delete all words", wrote a Chinese sage,
"and then you will have the true poster."
"There is no such thing as a statement."
"Am I asking too many questions?"

Correct, all quotes from our speakers,
who've logoed banks or drawn their fonts
from inmate scrawl. One's intrigued
by the tricolour bags of Hong Kong.

Can horses gallop on tomatoes?
Bien sûr! barked Breton's dog.
Cuban film will receive some remarks.
Meet an elephant crossed with a coffee pot.

The Botanical Garden, the Museum
of Natural History are their clients.
The Literature House. The Public Theater.
Please welcome this morning's designers.

Your Collages

Technicolor things
ice-climbing your walls
with drawing pins:

take the Amazon frog,
livid and slim-legged,
fingering a hotdog,

or the husky snout
splashing behind swimcaps.
There's a freedom to be found

in your knives and noses,
power-drills and courgettes
tumbling down Alpine slopes.

Your reading skids
from Soviet science fiction
to the sites of hominids,

as I sprawl at your side,
statue on white sheets,
dormant synapse

about to make links
under splicings that suggest
how chimeras might think.

A Note on the Door in the Land of No Phones

I came around and found today
your grey door under narcosis.
Rough-cut strata of paper
stared from the hook in the shadow.

The stairwell paint: cracked ice.
The lino: dug and furrowed.
Out in the East German early nineties
you were short of a sheepskin coat

but found one on the uneven pavement
of furniture and fashion,
restyling neighbours. Your architrave:
We Still Wash Up By Hand.

Gone to the park, I wrote,
Meeting at nine in Kommandantur.
The stub of the pencil slowed,
pendulum strung from the door.

And I'm glancing now through glass
at thin, medieval scribbling
beside the museum's gloss
that puts the scrawl into print.

The New Village

Next door, the planners move in
to the nineteenth century, emerge
into the trending twenty-first
and stroll the Atlantic rim.

Snow's on the roof. The cobbles
mumble with four-wheel drives,
their constant, continental drift
where the silk-weavers' looms have stopped.

We've decided to split into two,
but a flathunter's foot slides
over ice, as the temperatures rise.
Divided the calendar up too –

you get May, I march in March.
What year was the village first mentioned,
estate agent? Prices of land
contour and colour the chart.

New, they're saying, is old.
The agreements freeze and melt
where the white mulberries were felled,
now the land where we live has been sold.

Riding Home with Michel Foucault

At the corner of the evening screen
the seconds' decimal discourse
inverts the countdown of the genes.
The acrobatic pixels pause,

then scatter and land as a flock
above the platform's bustle
where the bright and broken dots
summon the orange shuttle.

I run for the doors
to take my temporary seat
and read the origin of laws.
The books beside me speak:

"Where are you now on the market?"
"Are you sure you're on the right diet?"
This State is my life, it asks me
to ride and read by night

and under the sun in the ceiling.
In the accepted world,
silence my slang as I steal
back to our flat from work,

head for the holed coin of the lock,
and from my wallet extract
the access card to the office.
This morning, across and apart,

two eyes were tracking the lectures
with an avian shade of concentration.
We were picking at the same conjectures
in our pair of varying translations,

while the driver watched from his cabin,
polo-necked, accelerating past
in the passages, looking happy
with his bald head and quick-witted glasses.

We sleep inside four circled walls,

one of them warm till nine or ten,
the others cool while birds – again! –
keep making anonymous calls.

Wall Two: the dimmed-up midday lamp
directs degrees across that steep
unconquered cliff that seems to keep
our peopled bookshelves free of damp.

At the third wall the rays all stop.
Stiff and prim, the thousand-fingered tree
frisks them down, and the year will see
that chestnut's printed pages drop.

Behind the last, our neighbours hide,
builders whose twilight shifts we hear.
And through that face we disappear
in the season's jacket, outside.

Le Monde diplomatique

It comes out like the moon
in its matt white skin
imprinted with tattoos,

emerging from the pile
of local and daily
clouds rambling the sky.

The frozen ground
is melting away.
The Wars of Africa
warm up the graphics.
Europeans dream revolt
in the lands of Che.

Outside, the flies are making
short-haul flights from stamen
to stamen on a great wall of ivy.

About a Country

My travelling mate's been telling me
about your woods and hills,
your favourite words and more

about your town that's two towns,
your school that's now two schools –
twin, simultaneous tunes –

about the tracks and roads
you keep to, the anti-personnel
pebbles washed into the reeds,

the hidden hate at every metre
(under the floorboards, the family
tools and oiled mortar),

your pair of identical languages,
serrated, needing interpreters
to coil the ceasefire lines,

snappable metal threads.
To strum your songs on the street
is to risk the telephone threats

from the furious apprentices
who hoot and whoop in the woods
with Kalashnikovs and clear spirits,

just off the road last seen
slicing two towns that receive
their equal servings of sun.

for Moon

At Haifa

Nobody here has directions
from the station up to the hilltop.
The cable car sets behind tower blocks,
and the Russians parade past our questions.

Near the open hand of the harbour,
Luther's language arcades oak doors,
but the Kaiser won't roll past once more
to wave at His colony. The Bahá'í gardens

steepen in their palm-tree terraces,
lush to the ridge, effusive and neat.
The convent watches the Phoenician sea
for the ships of the refugee-settlers

who hail the horizon of the Declared Land,
where workshops turn out interest and intrigue.
Stealth and stabbings do well in the fields.
New bricks, old bricks in old new hands.

A meticulous Bauhaus bakery where
the German they talk has a Dessau accent
and a third generation leaves and flies back
to the breathable, fearful air.

Khakassian Masks

1

The Tang soldiers pant up the grass
and arrest the first nomad they can find.
They mishear *Kyrgyz* and decide
they've found the land of *Khakas*.

2

You fling out the final expressions
you held as you posed in the graves
till the sunlight started to rain
on your faces again from the west.

3

Across the full moon's paleness
hung against a black background,
the blue and yellow, red and brown powder
paints rivers and brooks, lakes and plains.

4

Your eyelids arc like arrows,
each iris an immobile clock.
Each face a lake where a strong wind blows
a grin or grimace, grumpiness, shock.

5

Stately, serene and smooth,
half your head is history.
Your mate with the Maori swirls, his mouth
tight-clenched, has the cheeks of a weight-lifter.

6

Eyes down-turned, ears apart,
you assist your portrait artist.
A thick red spiral perfects your brow.
Death has become you. You can go now.

7

You mouth your sounds in a pond,
a side-hall in the House of Culture.
The Khans waded in with their script,
and the captions bubble in Russian.

8

Your two hundred oral epics trot off.
Look after the old. Look after the poor.
Dress well. Be sure to own a good horse.
But your tunes have turned into ethno-rock.

9

Your careers as potter or shaman
all end in plaster noses.
The two containers the earth discloses:
the impermeable clay and the cranium.

10

Blue and black, the eye pigment codes.
It's never advisable to own an abode
where empires finalize their borders
and genetics meets torch and sword.

11

Dream, and the narratives arrive.
There in the smoke, the souls rise.
The overtone moves in the grass;
the hooter haunts the smelting plant.

12

Your faces hold the republic's coins:
the molybdenum, grey and bright,
that fed the oceans with nitrogen,
great for evolution and alloys.

13

Opaque, brittle barite as well,
to weight the fluid that finds the oil.
Asbestos, tablecloth of Charlemagne,
to hold back the invading flames.

14

Beneath the grass we found your axeheads,
and tungsten, the heavy stone,
the glittering grey to shroud the cones
of our long-range waiting warheads.

15

The brown eagle's neck twitches
atop its moss-quiet megalith.
Above the long grass in a midday gale,
no higher resolution is available.

16

The megaliths bend with the wheat-ears
beneath the geostationary rain-clouds.
The rape plants raise their yellow flowers
to the wisps across online Siberia.

17

In the evening valleys' red spaces,
the megaliths display like crystals.
We can see our ancestors' chisels
in the pixels of the public domain.

18

Squinting a little from the saddle,
the red tunic no disguise,
leant on a table, trying on a smart hat,
these riders under the same skies.

Oblast

The wagtail's plumage a woodcut,
the sandbank a log
traffic balances along
between lagoon and Baltic
and into Lithuanian mists.

The bricks cohere to a *Kirche*,
squat and ziggurat-roofed.
The Word seconded to Slavic:
nave hung with fresh icons
now the interregnum
as a barn has passed.

They sow the alders
to halt the dance of the dunes,
the lagoon smooth as a salt plain.
Cattle gaze from the tarmac,
and a pig is loose in the village.
The coach will take us
under the turnpike
and out of the National Park.

The Milan Duomo

Like puffins nesting on their shit-white cliffs,
gargoyles peer out from under the spire tops,
where perching angels play dummies in shops.
Prophets and saints ascend on outside lifts.

The cross-vault spreads across a colonnade
of redwoods. Yes, the vestments of Christ's bride,
the Passion hoardings brand the faith: this side
of the Schism they like the visual aid –

five centuries of surplus value transform
into a thousand stories in stained glass.
Below, a tide of pews that waits for class.
The nave expresses the behavioural norm.

You're reminded that this is a place of prayer
by voices above, speaking in tongues. Shapes
of martyrdom conduct us to the apse,
far destination. Thank God for this chair.

The marble sermon sounds, and I could use
a career path from cardinal to saint,
when my skin's mummified, blotched with dark paint
and prone. Be sure I'm wearing my best shoes.

Great Uncle in the Great Unknown

The negative develops
on the downside,
in the solid heat and cumulus flies.
Cross-legged and goggled
in the black-and-white fifties,

you squat on ground whose stories
an empire shouts down,
as you wait for the wave with the desert
animals in a private costume
and a seat at a general rehearsal.

A dreaming roams the landscape,
television across a night yard.
The plume greets the spotter plane.
Dust and dose
bloom from centre to rim.

Ten years to write up the results
and no conclusion
in the four letters of the nucleotides.
It's beyond compensation,
an entry in the family genes.

Ode on a Bottle of Maotai

Undreamt-of content of 53%! –
slow fluid that thick white walls will hide,
like snow that holds a pond out of sight –
break the ice, let the spirit enter.

Only your weight can state what's left
with which to sprinkle the final banquet.
No Grecian face on your opaque flank,
but strokes in auspicious red. A lift

into sky from the drizzle and cold,
where, quadruple, you copy the boosters
of the national rocket, white bottles clustered
round a white column, bloated a hundredfold,

cathedral of an advert on the square,
while out on each production line
they reproduce your glassy wine.
Rip off the red plastic, friend, unscrew

that top! Now pour. Downstream of the Dam
the engineers have raised their toast,
a hint of vomit in its scent and taste:
Oh hold your drink and don't fall down.

Shanxi Tune

The forests bide rich periods
in drizzled, undated peat,
each pressing down a predecessor
and breathing in less and less.
Then the cavemen call with axes,
pulleys and wired explosives;
as the megatons roll into light,
the particulate matter flies.
Philosophers and officials
feel the bivalve fossils,
      their rilled CDs
      printed at sea.

The mining families of the loess
enter dynastic barrows.
As they drill, each syllable sounds
like a rising or sinking cloud.
With a carbon monoxide headache
and their paleolabour they shed
the cane that feeds the turbines
and powers the factory enzymes,
processed and broken
down to package over oceans
      to Rotterdams and Vancouvers
      in oblong balloons.

At Datong station, your feet
complain about the dark sleet,
as the macrophages engulf
the dust that digs into lungs,
and the scrubbed-down shift
ghost past. Out of the pit
one picks up his *sheng*, and starts
to blow through its shafts,
an orchestral, oscillating tone
that talks to fossil and stone,
      a local stream
      blown to the sea.

The Burbage Valley

Within the great gap which
no glaring text or image
could nudge the brain to envisage,
given the wind's gradations,
the solar degrees, the latent
unquarried space to leap into,

each international prospector
of the boulder's climbing wealth
makes a distant mica speck –
like a waste dump's compacted glitter –
on the cliff's fantastic grip,
its shape and balance and friction.

This is a place chalk hands
reach out and write a synapse,
where the gritstone neurones happen.
Make your Mark on the torn
anticline's castle, peer down
to the dip and a furry Dunsinane.

Surely, someone's inscribed
somewhere on rock these lines:
I am the ruler of Darbyshire.
My realms comprise Mam Tor's
crumpled road, the Cave of Thor,
Chee Dale, Stanage, Kinder Downfall.

Done with the events of the coast
in the air, the mud and stone
of the moorland's minor archipelago,
the foot-dangling raven
flaps down the path to the Iron Age
fort's rounded oration,

blanks the reed bunting,
and deaf to the zebra finch's
elaborate laboratory signals,
it heads for the gallery district's
graffitied alleys and the derelict
steel mills, the developing relicts.

The British Museum

Visitors are requested to rise
from the ground to the first floor where
they can blow through the halls and slide
down the marble and granite far stairs.

As you enter, please condense
to a raining, migrating population
of Pharaohs and Athenian goddesses
to stroll through the Gate of All Nations.

Then drift into the room of scripts
and spells to whisper in the bull's ear.
Learn about loans and land sales, sip
the slave's ration of beer.

Can you find the bits of bad Latin
on untouchable stone that spotlights warm
as they fall on the ragged patterns
of pots and schoolchild cuneiform?

Somewhere in this permanent exhibition
you'll meet a fired clay figurine
among fragments of empire and expedition
bequeathed by the Earls of Aberdeen:

whetstone, boneholder, sword and amulet,
ivory, clay, jade and flint.
Watch out for the spit of the Bactrian camel
from a nineteenth-century German print.

Ask the Urartians why their god
was a charging bull with wings.
The oil, the wine and the grain have gone,
but we know their demons were griffins.

How come these miniature bottles
are the record that remains –
the talking microfossils –
of the Sasanian perfume trade?

The obsidian migrates from lava to cloak
to here, black beetle under glass.
If you are looking for the nomad
milk-fermenters of Luristan,

walk under the solar surveillance and flash
and through the tribal cloud,
relief and seal, bowl and axe,
then down and past the way out.

From the Annals

Much as it's best to be wary
of those who rhyme on about Rome
and get their kicks from the Greeks –
Mussolini, the British Empire,
the drafters of Treaties Of Stars –
you can't beat the ancient Penguins
for the histories no Rushdie could better.

Suetonius: some would break limbs
tumbling from walls as they fled
incestuous Nero's incessant
compulsory public recitals.
Women would feign labour.
Men would pretend to be dead.

Or Tacitus (Nero again):
the rival who wanted more wine.
His boy took a taste.
He sipped it himself. Too warm!
(The henblane was in the cooling water.)

The Republic begins with a slave
running up to get Socrates to stop.

Separate State and Verse
and stick to the drink of the Germans.
Ban and burn the works of Plato.
Rethink the European heritage
of an economy managed by chains.

The Ex-Pat Gift Shop Owner Sells Up

The day I've handed over
my final Royal China,
no piper, band or liner
will bring me back to Dover.

No pumping, pompous brass'll
see me from the quay.
I'll simply leave the key
to my abandoned castle.

The swirling, slanting script –
no more shall it suggest
the products that are best
lie in this well-lit crypt,

relicts we should have sold.
Our Dundee cakes are chewy.
Our fudge has gone all gooey.
The jam has grown a mould.

Oh celebrat'ry mug!
No more shall your squat form
be filled up with that warm
and liquid daily drug.

So when the audit finds
that sales have gone too slack,
I'll haul in the Union Jack,
let fall the clanking blinds.

But that fine cloth shall not
be lost in a jumble sale.
I'll raise it at the tail
of my retirement yacht.

They Flick The Lights Back On

Matches and meetings are hard to clinch
when losers won't give up.
Out of your hands they try to wrench
that just-kissed FA Cup.
Out of your hands tug tug they wrench
decisions duly taken.
"Was that the way that that was meant?
The minutes are mistaken."

    It's tiring after twenty tries,
    just when you think you've won,
    and rest your legs and shut your eyes,
    they flick the lights back on.

"That last point you threw in, well I
can't follow it at all."
When faced with windows some will try
to brick back in a wall,
or volunteer their rearrangements
of chants already heard
until we hum them their new way
and silence has concurred.

    It's tiring after twenty tries,
    just when you think you've won,
    and rest your lungs and shut your eyes,
    they flick the lights back on.

"Let's check again around the table."
It isn't them and us,
but us and them that will retable
proposals to discuss
old fouls until we fall. Remark
adjacencies of chairs.
Although the landing looks all dark,
the whispers work the stairs:

> "It's tiring after twenty tries,
> just when you think you've won,
> and rest your lungs and shut your eyes,
> they flick the lights back on."

I've stood there too and taken aim,
missed in the penalty duels,
alone before the crowd in a game
where no one speaks their rules,
where people speak when they should listen,
and listen when they should speak,
and cheer too soon, where no one wins
world cups by being meek.

> It's tiring after twenty tries,
> just when they think they've won,
> and rest their legs, lungs, shut their eyes,
> you flick the lights back on.

The Transsylvanians at Supamolly, Berlin, 7 Jan 2012

Beyond the forest we go
back to the nineties squat scene,
the half-refurbished dream
awake in the occupied home,
the all-night cellar parties
and daylong kitchen meetings
with mates and ridiculous arses,

to the alternative dark.
The profit motive? Outside.
The glitzy mermaid presides
in papier-mâché over cast-
iron Mayan balustrades.
The happy fish on the ceiling
are swallowing notes and staves.

Fifteen years of surprise.
Old songs resoldered, the new
busting a fuse
under the filtered lights,
or moving the molten room.
In their rainbow spots,
the geographical tunes

crash-course us in Hungarian,
talking in keys and skins,
in deep, then higher strings.
In a hall that bans all chairs
the Friday night lives
meet and melt in the mosh.
András drops and dives

onto a factory of hands
conveying him round the rim,
as he demiquavers his violin.
Famous enough for fans,
not enough to ignore them.
I pass on the T-Shirt.
Once, another audience

took action and removed
the well-meant folding rows
to free the floor for those
melodies born acoustic,
that grew up amplified
and tour in my head – *Köszönöm!* –
in changing line-ups and times.

The Sock Exchange

Belt at my haunches,
in my sober clothes
I slope off at dawn
to rummage in funds
of rainbow stripes,
flimsy pull-ons
and Alpine hikers.

In Shanghai they're peeling away
skin-toned ankle-warmers.
In Tokyo they've pulled off
mittens with dedicated
holes for big toes.

It's only a pun of course,
copied by hosiers
in the financial centres.

Today, in emotional scenes,

scores of socks were reunited
for the first time in decades.

Salat Komplett

1

I get my lahmacun
where they belt out Turkish tunes
and *bitteschön* the orders.
They grill the flat round bread
and add red cabbage, lettuce,
onion on request. What sauce?
Mixed herbs and chilli, both.
No thanks, I don't want Coke.
The döner spit bulges and rises,
bee-hive slowly scorched.
No smiles, but I stay loyal
while they fold the piled-up circle
into a quiver of foil.
They belt out Turkish tunes
as I snatch my lahmacun,
descend to the platform
and go straight to work.

2

I get my hair needs seen to
half-listening to Baghdad TV,
where chlorophyll feels its way
up and around the mirrors,
above razors, gel and scissors.
I mount the throne, they tape
the top of my crimson robe,
and – careful of my earlobe –
a harvester hums across
the curving prairie. The nape
knows aftershave, and all
that growth gathers unsheaved
about the threshing floor.
And from the high-up screen
as we chat, *mujahideen*
is the word that escapes
beside the potplant leaves.

The Courtyard

No more shall my teeth sink into your falafel,
fingertips soak bread in your bowl of *foul*.

No more shall I ask you for an inlay of chilli,
to work in the pickled radish, that purple jewel.

Al-Mokhtar, you've abandoned your courtyard garden,
the shading colonnade and the cooling pool

just photographic tales behind parcel paper
veiling the windows. There's a sign of renewal –

BETTING SHOP. OPENING SOON! –
but your caliphate is under new rule.

Have your hands located better patrons?
I'm hungry. The market is cruel.

Fixing a Clock

This side of Nazareth Church
it's always five to twelve,
while where you're standing, waiting,
it's gone five minutes past.

Where the office voltage hums,
the seconds tap, the minutes peer,
our hours begin to hunch,

while under the station arches
a loitering truncheon trio
move on a man on crutches.

This side of Nazareth Church
it's always five past twelve,
while where you're standing, waving,
it's still five minutes to.

There must be stairs inside
to take us to the top
and fix the midday cogs,

or else we'll have to climb
into the wind and hang
at midnight from our hands.

An Update on the Status of Frost

Windows make fine translators
in cold, white morning light.
Gingko leaves, barbed wire lines,
rivers when viewed from space.

About our future, I would say:
the management of forests,
new languages of frost,
the constant labour of status.

Disturbance

Although I can't smell the dust
that flees and flies from the crater
up to the galleries and cancels
all bets across the great surface,
the doctors are grounded in Toronto.
Paul Cooke is stuck in Berlin.

Beautiful field of Schönefeld,
the crows are shunning your furrows.
As we stumble out of the cellar
and into the drunken sunlight,
our ears are an empty stadium,
minus the kerosene singing.

I'm driving inside a black cloud.
My foot is moving in the soot.
I'm opening the unlocked door
of your low, Icelandic home,
below the immobilized sky,
even though the aroma of ash

won't penetrate the crystals.
Amid the morning airspace,
antiquity drones once more,
a break in the global airlift.
Around the yard the blackbirds
are squawking their announcements.

The Financial Ocean

You tack out on the grey-suited waves,
the renewable billows in the hoisted sail
of your market-going catamaran that rises
and crashes while Swindon Marina recedes,
pinned on the New Riviera, between
the hill-hugging call centres of Bristol
and the songbird wharves of the Capital, first
to faint as the crisis seeped in. Your colleagues
have left their strip-lit offices and Outlook meetings
to wave your keels off. Even the CEO
has tasked her assistant, who starts to click mails
as the white horizon begins to delete your sail
and you turn off down the motorways of the whales.

You lean to tack your operational platform
to one side, on course for the tropics and exotics.
Stocked to the ceiling with bonds and policies,
the pension plan in the locker, a larder
of complex products to swap with peoples
whose coasts you'll swing your feet onto, you've nodded
and neighed on Business Lunch, the full roll-out.
Before you, blue sky and the sponsored biplanes,
test jets that raced ahead of the boom;
futures cross oceans in the stratosphere.
You'll remain in communion with the relay stations
as you groove the waters of the fish nations
and movements in the market slew your navigation.

Five days out, clouds curl and blacken, the wind thickens.
Ten, and you glimpse death's old derivative, the albatross.
You put in at some rocks the satnav missed and meet
a culture counting shells round a necklace of islands,
facing storms without disaster securities.
On this voyage to the Indies, the share winds
hurry your course. But as your keels round
the Cape of Crisis, an obscenity filter
forgets your text to head office. Inside the ring road
your colleagues have short-sold your chances
at their screens and filed the new stakes
with the sea regulators, but CC you in by mistake,
a message you read into your investment's wake.

The Travellers

They chased Atlantics and Pacifics
on steamships, clutching journals, keen
to touch the grit, the stone specifics
of the great tide their friends had seen
and sung. On morning strolls they'd stop
to ask when lunch was. On that trek
by chart and choice they hoped to swap
their portholes for views from the deck

on the moving, moon-hurled waves.
They'd swirled the soup, seen miners shot –
it was time to drill seams from caves.
The issue now not why but what.
Hymn handouts? No. They'd disengage
from nineteenth-century meals and missions
and steam to the twentieth, the age
of quick, economic fissions,

light bulbs, literacy campaigns,
inoculations. Now they docked
beneath the whirring, swerving planes
overhead with their claws that dropped
whistling payloads in civil wars
and interventions, direct hits.
The Comrades locked the hate-shocked doors,
then looked out from trenches and pits.

Traveller, you too bound up a wound,
but now you saw the chimneys rise,
the heirdoms fall, your eardrums tuned
to national sounds. Bridges split skies.
The end started, the start had ended,
the contradictions dropped behind.
But though you tried your best to spend it,
your past gained interest in the Comrade's mind.

You met them all, the people's leaders,
and some became the leader's people,
reporting what was right for readers
(the mattress diary blabbed your scruple).
The daylit room slowly grew dim:
you criticized yourself, or drank,
now "foreign" seemed a synonym
for "suspect", stood through trial and camp.

If and when you coughed and limped out,
you still wrote books for folks back home
with photos of tower blocks, about
your foster homes on steppe and loam,
ploughed out again a trenchant page,
translated, and received the young.
The TB purged, you died of age
in chosen exile, on one lung.

Meeting the Family

Take me to greet your relatives
emplaced around the low hills,
covering their ears against familiar
chatter on the New Year visit.

Let's bump out there to inspect them,
the old spring-rolled into back seats, the young
clutching the sides of a bare-backed truck,
surfing the potholes, next

to arrive with an hour's supply
of Gatling Gun crackers in the breeze,
to mow down a Square of Heavenly Peace,
put five generations on trial.

Here we are. Your ancestral homes
are of earth and tufted with grass.
Like wriggling dragons, the annual paths
aren't happy or sad. Let's burn our banknotes.

Your eldest brother has the farmhouse.
The second, the haulage firm, Audi,
and Country & Western ringtone.
Your sister, the unspecified business.
You have the punk drumkit.

Third cousin, a pleasure to meet you
and feast in a room of resemblances
and filling, revolving tables. Thanks!
We're glad to be here among the iron trees,

where I might sink into the earthquake zone
and mime the unrelated individual
when centuries hence they find the pit
and my DNA here in the chicken bones.

The fuzzy dashes fuzzy dots

tapped out on mitochondrial blots
show Lower Saxons riding tractors
share a mound of genetic factors
with local, broken skeletons
found round hearths for forging bronze.

Only the bovine liked to roam,
while most of us just worked from home.
But still, our longitudinal tests
across the millennia suggest
that even those who don't migrate
across the mountains may mutate:

the old man in the next door flat,
brownshirt, turned Christian Democrat,
then Social. Oh he drank drank drank.
His bedroom sink, though, always stank
no matter if he'd tapped in ash
or stumbled towards a night-time slash.

Oh I don't know. Recall Doreen,
who dated Nazis, took a plane
to Shanghai from her Saxon town
Berliners know is brown brown brown.
She changed her views on good physique
and bagged a bloke from Mozambique.

Nobody's Mate

Ah, Nobody's Mate,
I believe we met
in a Moravian cellar.
Not even a slur
of a greeting slipped
from your caved-in lips.
Brittle and tanned,
your monastic hands
clasping towards God,
you weren't looking good:
bone-blind, your face
depleted of all faith.

It seems you've still got
strong media contacts,
hang around hospitals,
get off on statistics.
Qualified sniper,
you're totally fine
with machines that make
epidemics mechanical.
I know it's your vans
that have snatched my friends,
but all your quarters
are ex-territorial.

For some, you're a wall
or a leaping white wolf,
a sinking cloud,
sound of the first clod,
or you sulk in the darkest
recess of the disco,
where no one will talk to you.
Have you been stalking me? –

I sense you underfoot
among your leased fields
at the leafy edges
of Bohemian villages,
or revving alongside
my commuting bicycle.
Excuse me. There are projects
and friends I've neglected,
so I can't stand around.
I hope you understand.

The Forester leads beneath the trees,

as a father weeps behind his shades.
Then a CD plays
as thoughts fall on the urn.
We used to call this a return.
Hug and hold
a bare-shirted shoulder.
Ritual keeps to the road
then swerves: no prayers. Instead,
a letter to the dead.
Nor flowers. A slice of trunk
the lid that ivy rings
like pumice round a crater.
Here is a sample grave
that no one needs
to tend. The rest
we'll leave to nature.

The Shelves

Perhaps one morning
you'll review
the data on love,

when the research that trickled
into the articles
on altruistic genes
and generalized reciprocity
from card games for cash
won't seem enough,

the day you leave home
for the home and find
your heirs have dealt you a hand
of new shelves
with all your papers
roughly
in the right order.

Escape

Should any Clause
herein be duff,
stuffed with flaws
that whimper and yelp,
their limps enough
to preclude all help,
should there be omissions
or growling decisions,
these shall not affect
the bones then left
but rather be chased
off and replaced
by the calls the Parties
would have howled out
if they'd known from the start
what they were barking about.

Acknowledgements

Some of these poems have previously appeared, sometimes in earlier versions, in *B O D Y*, *Fuselit*, *Kumquat*, *Shearsman*, *SNOW*, *Tears in the Fence*, *The Interpreter's House*, *The Ofi Press* and *The Prague Revue*. Thanks to the editors concerned, as well as to Justin Quinn and Ben Borek. 'The Burbage Valley' was written as part of the artist Paul Evans' *The Seven Wonders* project: seven-wonders.org – with thanks to Paul, Brian Lewis, Nikki Clayton and Mark Goodwin.

Also by Alistair Noon:

At the Emptying of Dustbins (Oystercatcher)
In People's Park (Penumbra)
Animals and Places (Longbarrow)
Long and Other Short Poems (Silkworms Ink; e-chapbook)
Some Questions on the Cultural Revolution (Gratton Street Irregulars)
Out of the Cave (Calder Wood)
Across the Water (Longbarrow)
Swamp Area (Longbarrow)
Earth Records (Nine Arches)
Surveyors' Riddles (Sidekick, with Giles Goodland)

As translator:

The Last Drop: Versions of August Stramm (Intercapillary; e-chapbook)
16 Poems. Monika Rinck (Barque)
The Bronze Horseman. Alexander Pushkin (Longbarrow)

As editor:

Seán Rafferty. A Revue (Intercapillary; e-chapbook)